Hidden in God's Heart

Also by Lisa Aré Wulf

Reaching for God's Hand
40 Reflections to Deepen Your Faith Journey

Enfolded in God's Arms
40 Reflections to Embrace Your Inner Healing

On a Quest for Christ
Tracing the Footsteps of Your Spiritual Journey

Silent Moments with God Series

Hidden in God's Heart

40 Reflections to
Draw You Close to Christ

Lisa Aré Wulf

Spiritual Formation House
Colorado Springs, Colorado
www.spiritualformationhouse.com

Scripture quotations marked (NIV) are taken from THE HOLY BIBLE, NEW INTERNATIONAL VERSION®, NIV® Copyright © 1973, 1978, 1984, 2011 by Biblica, Inc.® Used by permission of Zondervan. All rights reserved worldwide. www.zondervan.com The "NIV" and "New International Version" are trademarks registered in the United States Patent and Trademark Office by Biblica, Inc.™

Scripture quotations marked (NLT) are taken from the Holy Bible, New Living Translation, copyright © 1996, 2004, 2007, 2013, 2015 by Tyndale House Foundation. Used by permission of Tyndale House Publishers, Inc., Carol Stream, Illinois 60188. All rights reserved.

Cover Design by Fresh Vision Design
Interior Design by Wood Nymph Creations
Cover Photograph by Lepusinensis (Depositphotos)
Author Photograph by Katie Corinne Photography

Publisher's Cataloging-in-Publication data

Names: Wulf, Lisa Are, 1950-, author.
Title: Hidden in God's heart : 40 reflections to draw you close to Christ / Lisa Are Wulf.
Series: Silent Moments with God
Description: Colorado Springs, CO: Spiritual Formation House, 2022.
Identifiers: LCCN: 2022907324 | ISBN: 978-1-938042-20-1 (hardcover) | 978-1-938042-19-5 (paperback) | 978-1-938042-24-9 (large print) | 978-1-938042-21-8 (Kindle) | 978-1-938042-22-5 (epub) | 978-938042-23-2 (audio)
Subjects: LCSH Christian women--Prayers and devotions. | Christian women--Religious life. | Christian living. | Devotional exercises. | Devotional calendars. | BISAC RELIGION / Christian Living / Devotional
Classification: LCC BV4832.2 .W84 2022 | DDC 242/.3--dc23

Published by Spiritual Formation House™
3154 Vickers Dr.
Colorado Springs, CO 80918
www.spiritualformationhouse.com

Printed in the United States of America

To all who seek God

Contents

Abiding with God

Acknowledgements

I am delighted to thank these very special friends whose contributions and support for this book have been invaluable:

My fabulous editor, Kim McCauley, whose expertise, patience, and friendship were indispensable to this effort.

My two great test readers, Jan Malvern and Jerusha Goebel, whose insights and encouragement refined and shaped this offering.

My excellent proofreader, Susan Defosset, whose eagle eye carefully combed through every inch of the manuscript.

My wonderful husband, Calvin, for his sage advice, encouragement, and patience through endless readings and conversation.

Thanks to each one. This book has become a reality because of you!

The Journey Begins

How lovely is your dwelling place, LORD Almighty!
My soul yearns, even faints, for the courts of the LORD;
my heart and my flesh cry out for the living God.
Psalm 84:1-2 (NIV)

Picture two hearts entwined forever—yours and God's, united for all eternity. You feel happy. You feel safe. You feel loved. You know this bond will never break. Wait! Is this real, or just a delightful daydream?

Okay, so let's explore another sweet scenario. Imagine you are visiting God's home. You and Jesus stroll through the garden, then enjoy a leisurely lunch on the patio. In the afternoon, you linger at the pond as he listens attentively to your troubles. An evening snack by the fireplace caps off an idyllic time. What a wonderful day, just you and Jesus together. So, is this a dream? It doesn't have to be.

Our souls long for the peace that only Christ offers. Difficulties and dilemmas separate us from him. Daily life is a struggle. Relationships are strained. Even spending a few minutes in prayer is a stretch. But keep looking for Jesus. He is always by your side—ready to listen, console, and guide.

Hidden in God's Heart: 40 Reflections to Draw You Close to Christ is part of the Silent Moments with God series. Each chapter illustrates a typical challenge in growing close to him. The writings are gathered in four groups:

Connecting with God
Walking with God
Growing with God
Abiding with God

Each reflection begins with a Scripture verse, brief devotional, and some questions to consider. A second Bible quote and a short prayer are included. Be sure to take a minute to journal your thoughts.

Don't miss the special section in each chapter titled, "A Silent Moment with God." It's important to pause and sit quietly. Open your mind to hear what he is saying to you. Your path to Jesus is personal. Your experience is unique. Each devotional approaches the spiritual life from a different perspective, yet a common rainbow emerges from the many facets of this Christian prism.

The journey to God's heart involves dedication—lots of it! How do we build an enduring relationship? We set aside time. We ponder life issues together. We honor our commitments to him.

This road is not easy or problem-free, but no matter where we are on the pathway, he's right there, eager to lead us home.

One thing I ask from the LORD, this only do I seek:
that I may dwell in the house of the LORD
all the days of my life,
to gaze on the beauty of the LORD . . .
Psalm 27:4 (NIV)

May you find peace, joy, and contentment on your journey to God's heart.

Lisa

Connecting with God

❧

Each day we start anew, striving
to be ever more like Christ.

Waiting and Watching

Whoever serves me must follow me;
and where I am, my servant also will be.
John 12:26a (NIV)

The young man had a dream. He wanted to cook. But merely learning food prep wasn't enough. He set his sights on becoming a master chef in a first-class restaurant. With few opportunities and no money for tuition, he apprenticed himself to his idol, an international culinary artist.

For three years, more than a thousand days, he stood close by his teacher and watched. That's all he did—standing and watching, day after day. Later, he graduated to the next level, preparing meals by himself at home. Sometimes it worked. Sometimes it didn't. But he persevered. Finally, the young man finished his apprenticeship and was recognized by all as a gourmet chef.

This story could also be about Christian faith. Of course, this isn't an exact comparison because we can't graduate to "be Jesus." Yet new awareness is gained through standing and watching. We examine his life, view him in action, and ponder his deeds. Perhaps this is how we grow in Christlikeness.

Then, after studying his every move, it's time to venture forth to serve others. As we imitate Jesus, sometimes our efforts are fruitful. Sometimes they're not. But even then, we have not failed. Each unsuccessful attempt yields important clues for our upcoming pursuits. We're free to start anew, striving to become ever more like him.

Through it all, God smiles at our less-than-perfect experiments. As a parent picks up a child who has fallen, he dusts us off and sets us back on our feet, chuckling as he looks forward to our next adventure.

Imitate God, therefore, in everything you do,
because you are his dear children.
Live a life filled with love,
following the example of Christ.
Ephesians 5:1-2a (NLT)

Be Still
for a
Silent Moment with God

Digging Deeper

How do you feel about standing and watching Jesus for a time?

What do you see him doing that attracts you? Why?

In what ways could you begin to imitate him in your life?

Prayer for Today

Waiting and watching for a thousand days sounds impossible! So glad it's not what you're asking, God. But I am trying my best to "do as you do." As I mirror your actions out in the world, my efforts might work. They might not. But I always feel your love and encouragement. Help me continue walking with you forever. Amen.

Your Thoughts

⅌

As we bask in God's presence,
the world becomes a little brighter.

Presence

You will seek me and find me
when you seek me with all your heart.
Jeremiah 29:13 (NIV)

During the third century, a kindred group of Christians moved to the Egyptian desert. Leaving everything behind, they lived alone or in small clusters, tirelessly pursuing God. Men who were admired for their wisdom were called Abba. An insightful and holy woman was referred to as Amma.

One day, a hermit came to visit his Abba. They sat together in silence until the visitor left. An observer asked why the Abba didn't speak to his guest. He replied, "If he gains nothing by simply being in my presence, how then will he benefit by hearing my words?"

The first step to knowing God is to be present with him. In the beginning, this is enough. As our hearts become open and available, studying his word can be deeply satisfying. But without a receptive center, his promises just bounce around like ping-pong balls.

Letting go and resting in God's presence isn't easy. It takes effort and perseverance. Here are a couple ideas to try:

Consider listening—truly listening—as Jesus whispers his thoughts to you. Carve out a special time of silence, setting aside the noise and chaos. Even a few minutes a day will help you rest in his heart.

Or take him with you everywhere you go. Search for him as you drive to work, clean the house, or hang out with friends. Where is he? Can you place him in the room? Sense him in a flower? Or feel him tenderly clasp your hand?

As you bask in God's presence, the world becomes a little brighter. Look—he's right around the corner. Run and meet him!

Lead me by your truth and teach me,
for you are the God who saves me.
All day long I put my hope in you.
Psalm 25:5 (NLT)

Be Still
for a
Silent Moment with God

Digging Deeper

Do you feel God's presence with you? How?

In what other ways could you open yourself to him?

How do you sense him beckoning to you?

Prayer for Today

I long to feel your presence, God. But clutter and clatter keep getting in the way. Help me slow down and hold a silent space for us—just you and me. Open my eyes to see you in everything I do. Let's walk hand-in-hand into the horizon, together forever. Amen.

Your Thoughts

❧

Whatever our troubles,
we long to run to God's arms.

REFLECTION 3

Who Moved?

The LORD is near to all who call on him,
to all who call on him in truth.
Psalm 145:18 (NIV)

He jumped into the driver's seat as his wife settled in on the passenger side. Soon they were cruising along in their classic car, the one with the long bench seat. She looked wistfully out the window. "Remember back when we were dating—how we would drive for hours in this car, sitting close and holding hands? I sure miss it. What happened?"

"I didn't move," he replied.

We've all been there in our spiritual lives, haven't we? Some days, we feel inseparable from Jesus. We stroll side-by-side, talking, laughing, and even sharing tears. But then something happens. We sense a distance, our closeness vanishes, and everyday life seems drab.

God didn't move—we did. But why? Perhaps an accident or serious illness overwhelmed us. Or maybe issues at work or in relationships diverted our attention. It could be just the dailiness of reality catching up. No matter what the cause, our chaos swept us farther and farther from him.

And now the slow, meandering drift begins. Our prayer time doesn't seem important anymore, and our souls become dry. We no longer hear God's voice or sense his presence. Gradually, our Christian pursuits are displaced by other activities. Simply put, we've moved.

It is common to go through periods when Jesus seems far away. But whatever the situation, we long to return to him—to reunite and jump into his arms again. It's not too late to stop and make a U-turn. Let's run in his direction until he holds our hands in his once more.

"Look! I stand at the door and knock.
If you hear my voice and open the door, I will come in,
and we will share a meal together as friends."
Revelation 3:20 (NLT)

Be Still
for a
Silent Moment with God

Digging Deeper

Do you feel a little distant from God these days? If so, how?

What may be causing this?

How could you move close to him again?

Prayer for Today

Sometimes I don't feel close to you, God. You seem so far off, up in the ether somewhere. But I know you didn't move—I did. Somehow, I drifted away, choosing to spend my time elsewhere. Help me slow down and connect with you again. Let's walk side-by-side forever. Amen.

Your Thoughts

⁔

Take time today
for a leisurely walk with Jesus.

Peace Like a River

And the peace of God,
which transcends all understanding,
will guard your hearts and your minds
in Christ Jesus.
Philippians 4:7 (NIV)

Sitting next to a quiet, tranquil river, I was alone except for a solitary cow in the distance. The chilly air grew warm as the sun beamed down. I felt a profound sense of peace.

The water meandered lazily downstream—no hurry, no rush, just a soft, languid movement, constant like the earth itself. Nature pressed on in silence, unhurried by human fuss and commotion, reminding me that season follows season, year follows year.

I heard Jesus speaking earnestly about my frantic busyness, asking that I live at his pace. He mentioned my many commitments, my rushing back and forth, and the exhaustion that inevitably results. He whispered, "It's time to stop," as he urged me to carve out a breathing space for the two of us.

Could I do it? Could you do it? Soaking up sunlight by a creek on a lazy afternoon is one thing. Completely changing our lives is quite another. If we gave up our hard-driving lifestyle, how would we provide for ourselves? Catastrophe looms in the imagination. Panic sets in as we fear the worst.

But if we don't stop, we'll miss out on far more. It's vital that we take time to walk with Jesus, so we can hear his voice of wisdom as we weigh opportunities.

Most of us do too much. We want to "make it happen," personally and in our careers. Yet let's not forget that river gliding along the rocks, calm and serene. Nothing can stop it. Perhaps our real job is to flow with God—nothing more, nothing less.

> *You will keep in perfect peace*
> *all who trust in you,*
> *all whose thoughts are fixed on you!*
> *Isaiah 26:3 (NLT)*

Be Still
for a
Silent Moment with God

Digging Deeper

What is God telling you about the pace of your life?

Could you make changes? What are they?

In what ways will this bring you closer to God?

Prayer for Today

God, I'm so tired of rushing here and there. When I take a silent moment by the river, I feel my body and soul relax like a giant exhale. Could I live at the pace of a tranquil stream? Let me rest deeply in you as we leisurely stroll forever down the river of your grace. Amen.

Your Thoughts

౿

Jesus longs to sit quietly with us,
strengthening our sacred bond.

At Your Service

"I am the vine; you are the branches.
If you remain in me and I in you,
you will bear much fruit;
apart from me you can do nothing."
John 15:5 (NIV)

Serving God is so much fun! No matter where our interests and talents lie, we have loads of options. Between leading Bible studies and dishing out food at the soup kitchen, the calendar fills up, and we feel good about ourselves. Anyone can see that we're doing important work for our Lord.

This sounds wonderful, and I'm sure he appreciates our efforts. But there's a difference between being committed to God and being committed to our service for God. While devoting ourselves to "godly" activities, we may completely miss the reason for our service—Jesus himself.

Why do we get caught up in activity? Maybe because it's simpler. Ministry tasks keep us busy while giving a sense of accomplishment. We have a chance to be powerhouse Christians—leaders in the church and giants of the faith. With such an outstanding resumé, who would ever question our relationship with Jesus?

Probably no one—except Jesus himself. While we run here and there, serving on this committee and teaching that class, he patiently waits. He longs to sit quietly together, strengthening our sacred bond. While he appreciates all we do for him, what he truly wants is us!

This is a universal struggle. We're always tempted to do just a bit more, and yet this kind of doing is likely more about you and me than Jesus. If we want to show our devotion, let's shift gears, refocus, and spend time with him.

Jesus replied, "All who love me will do what I say.
My Father will love them,
and we will come and make
our home with each of them."
John 14:23 (NLT)

Be Still
for a
Silent Moment with God

Digging Deeper

How much time do you spend doing things for God, versus simply being with God?

In what ways might you alter that balance?

Could you ask Jesus to help and advise you on making this change? How?

Prayer for Today

I'm so busy, God. Ministry is a never-ending task. But something's missing. I've lost the joy of our relationship. In fact, some days I hardly see you at all. Let's just sit on the porch and sip a little iced tea together. I'd love that, and I'll bet you would too. Amen.

Your Thoughts

The longer we linger with Jesus,
the closer we become.

Any Dumb Bee

. . . faith comes from hearing the message,
and the message is heard
through the word about Christ.
Romans 10:17 (NIV)

Let's ponder for a moment about bees. A conference speaker once mused, "Any dumb bee knows not to go to a closed flower." In other words, open flowers are more receptive.

Seventeenth-century author Thomas Brooks wrote, "It is not the bee's touching of the flower that gathers honey, but her abiding for a time on the flower that draws out the sweet." The bee that stays the longest gets the tastiest nectar.

Do these two comparisons have anything in common? Yes—in a roundabout way. The first one could have implications for sharing our faith. How joyful it is to speak to someone with a willing and attentive spirit. Our conversation is mutual, rewarding, and fruitful. But when minds are shut tightly like clenched fists, moving on to more fertile ground is sometimes our best option. Likewise, we must keep our own ears and minds open to listen for God's voice.

The second quote contains a more profound truth. The longer we linger with Jesus, the more vividly we experience him. It's important to read the Bible and study his life. Yet, although much is learned through Scripture, as Brooks went on to explain, "It is not he that reads most, but he that meditates most, that will prove the choicest, sweetest, wisest and strongest Christian."

Listening yields the intimacy we crave. Whether we call it prayer, contemplation, or meditation, the outcome is the same. Sustained times of talking back and forth with God strengthens our bond.

So, what have we learned from bees? Know where to go and how long to stay!

'Call to me and I will answer you
and tell you great and unsearchable
things you do not know.'
Jeremiah 33:3 (NIV)

Be Still
for a
Silent Moment with God

Digging Deeper

Are you a receptive person? In what ways?

Do you sense that God is trying to get your attention? How?

Can you set aside a regular time just to listen? When?

Prayer for Today

I've always considered myself an open and receptive person, God. But too often I forget about you, failing to set aside time and space for us. Daily life overtakes me and crowds you out. Help me slow down and listen—really listen—to you. I know we will have wonderful times together, just you and me. Amen.

Your Thoughts

৵

Jesus is up ahead—
let's lovingly pursue him.

The Third Alternative

But the fruit of the Spirit is love, joy, peace,
forbearance, kindness, goodness,
faithfulness, gentleness and self-control.
Galatians 5:22-23a (NIV)

What's the best way to attract others to our faith? Two methods are often mentioned.

The first option is to talk openly about our beliefs. For those with the gift of evangelism, this solution is simple. But it can be super scary for the rest of us. Many would sooner run for the hills than to speak up.

Doing good deeds is another way to express our faith. Some dedicate themselves to caring for those less fortunate. Their work is vital, and yet, the belief that underpins these acts may never be revealed.

Let's consider a third alternative—just being. Have you

ever met someone who seems to have God's ear, and he has theirs? Jesus shines through their eyes. Their calm demeanor reflects a bottomless pool of spiritual depth. You're intrigued and inexplicably attracted to your new friend's serenity. Whatever he or she has, you want it too.

Where does this visible peace come from? Third-alternative folks integrate faith deep into their souls. They see Jesus in the distance and lovingly pursue him. They listen carefully as he whispers in their ears. They reverently pattern their lives after his. Their spirits are deepened and transformed through years of prayer and Scripture study.

So, what about you? If you're drawn to such a person, maybe God is sending you a message. Could he be asking you to walk toward the third alternative? If so, countless others may be brought to Christ through your example.

Why not ask Jesus today about what this option might look like in your life? Your question would delight him!

Make every effort to live in peace
with everyone and to be holy;
without holiness no one will see the Lord.
Hebrews 12:14 (NIV)

Be Still
for a
Silent Moment with God

Digging Deeper

Do you struggle with presenting your faith to others? In what ways?

How could you live the third-alternative life?

What is God whispering in your ear about this possibility?

Prayer for Today

I know people who seem to radiate your love, God. Peace and serenity shine from inside their souls. I can tell by their spiritual lives that they "really mean it." I want this too. It's a long path, but please help me begin today. Show me the way toward a deep and lasting relationship with you. Amen.

Your Thoughts

෨

Are we too busy reading about God
to actually know him?

Read All About It

"I love all who love me.
Those who search will surely find me."
Proverbs 8:17 (NLT)

I'm not old enough to remember the real thing, but I've seen films portraying young boys on street corners, hawking the newspapers. "Extra, extra! Read all about it," they shouted, hoping provocative headlines would sell more papers. That was a great strategy back then, but a fresh perspective is in order for today's Christian.

Studying, understanding, and applying the Bible is essential. That's why Bible studies are so popular. Brave believers even wade into theology books, trying their best to decipher God's Word. We're all spiritual sponges, absorbing everything we can. But are we so busy reading about God that we don't actually know God?

Grasping the basic tenets of our faith is crucial. But the object of this knowledge, Jesus Christ, is even more significant. We may discover countless details about him, but it's not the same as recognizing his face or hearing his voice.

A strong personal relationship with Jesus takes years to develop. We need time to be alone in his presence—time to talk with him about our lives, joys, and challenges, plus time to silently consider his answers. This is rather like having a famous friend. You could choose to read about her adventures in the headlines, or maybe you prefer coffee one-on-one. Which creates a closer connection?

Let's soak up all we can and not skimp on Bible study, keeping in mind that a rich and abiding sense of God's spirit is equally important. And here's the good news: we never need to choose between facts and relationships. Why not just take both?

My sheep listen to my voice;
I know them, and they follow me.
John 10:27 (NIV)

Be Still
for a
Silent Moment with God

Digging Deeper

Which describes you—knowing a lot about Jesus, knowing him personally, or both?

How could you convert your "book knowledge" to a deeper relationship?

He is holding out his hand to you. How will you respond?

Prayer for Today

I've read so many books about you, God, and have been super faithful in my Bible study. It's all been great, but something's missing. I long for a close and cozy relationship—just you and me. Help me make space in my life for you. Let's get to know each other. There's not a minute to waste! Amen.

Your Thoughts

໖

Listening to God's voice
is always our best response.

We Know What We Know

Whoever belongs to God
hears what God says.
John 8:47a (NIV)

You hear a troubling opinion, perhaps through the media or while talking with a friend, and it throws you off mentally. Why is the comment disturbing? And how will you handle it? The scene often plays out in one of two ways.

You may sit quietly, listening to beliefs that are opposite from those you've held for a long time. You don't challenge them, but suppress your own truth instead. No matter how far-fetched the conversation, you respond with a weak, timid smile.

Or perhaps you are so convinced of your own point of view that you immediately axe the other person's opinion. Even if it contains undeniable facts, that's irrelevant.

You accept none of it, rejecting the idea and sometimes the person too.

Is God nudging you forward through a message offered by someone else? He's been known to whisper new ideas through the mouths of family and friends. Then again, he may want you to hang onto your own thoughts, even in the face of another's strongly held belief.

Which is the best response? Should you change your mind? Stay the course? Re-think your position? If you are not really sure, it's best to ask Jesus first.

Being open-minded and willing to look at various perspectives is an admirable trait. So is standing firm in our own certainty, even against strong opposition. The trick is to keep focused on God's voice. We can remain unruffled in our reactions when we abide by the truth that he speaks personally to each of us. At our core, we will know what we know. Let's hold fast to his reality!

Your own ears will hear him.
Right behind you a voice will say,
"This is the way you should go,"
whether to the right or to the left.
Isaiah 30:21 (NLT)

Be Still
for a
Silent Moment with God

Digging Deeper

What do you do when someone expresses a belief that differs from yours?

How does this make you feel?

In what ways are you listening for God's soft, gentle whisper to you?

Prayer for Today

I know my beliefs are solid. But when my ideas are challenged, I waver. What should I do? Speak to me, God. Keep me open to new thoughts as I continue along the path you've chosen for me. Whisper your guidance as we hold this delicate balance. Amen.

Your Thoughts

⊱

It's hard to make room for God.
But we must!

Catching Up

"In repentance and rest is your salvation,
in quietness and trust is your strength . . . "
Isaiah 30:15 (NIV)

The special day finally arrived. How thrilling to attend a global ministry meeting. The man lived in a remote, rural settlement with his South American Guarani tribe. When the bus pulled up to his hut, he climbed aboard for the four-hour journey to Asunción, Paraguay.

As teacher and author Donald Clymer wrote, "Upon arrival, he was found sitting by himself in a corner. After nearly an hour had passed, a group of curious church leaders approached him to ask him if he needed anything. 'No thanks,' he said. 'It's just that the ride from my village to Asunción was so fast and furious that I am sitting here waiting for my soul to catch up with the rest of me.'"

This man's explanation reflects a modern-day spiritual struggle. Our world is all about hurry, hurry, hurry. Do this now. No, do this instead. Why aren't we finished yet? Our lives are a never-ending sprint to a non-existent finish line. There are achievements to pursue and possessions to accumulate. Round and round we turn, spinning out of control.

But what about our souls? They curl up in the shadows, anxious for the whirring to stop. Occasionally they venture forth, seeking quiet, searching for the still, small voice of God. Will they catch up and find tranquility—or drown in noise again?

Jesus didn't create you for the hurry-up life. Consider slowing down. Sit with him for a spell. Hear him whisper words of comfort as he pulls you close. In our fast-paced, results-oriented lives, it's hard to make room for God. But we simply must!

"My Presence will go with you,
and I will give you rest."
Exodus 33:14b (NIV)

Be Still
for a
Silent Moment with God

Digging Deeper

When has your soul struggled to catch up with the rest of you? Describe.

How could you carve out some quiet times for your spirit?

What might Jesus whisper to you during these moments together?

Prayer for Today

I know I'm too busy, God. My life is overloaded—too much to do and too many places to go. By society's standards, I am nothing without achievements and wealth. But I wonder. Is this what you want for me? No, I don't think so. Help me slow down to listen—really listen—to you. Amen.

Your Thoughts

Walking with God

୭

Finding a quiet moment with God
can be a challenge.

Turtle Speed

*Devote yourselves to prayer with an
alert mind and a thankful heart.*
Colossians 4:2 (NLT)

Why is surfing the Internet more fun than prayer? Why is a mountain hike more enticing than Bible reading? Why does just about anything seem cooler than talking with God?

Okay, these statements don't actually describe you. But consider this all-too-familiar scenario. You decide to carve out a few minutes a day to focus on Jesus. You really want to build a strong and growing connection with him. But your life is hectic. When evening comes, you're worn out.

So, you tumble into bed, vowing to begin anew tomorrow. Then the daily grind catches you in its grip again, and your pledge is forgotten. Today didn't turn out any better than yesterday, and you feel defeated.

Finding a quiet moment with God is challenging, even for the most seasoned saints. Throughout history, most have struggled to develop a consistent prayer habit. Some days were fruitful. Other days, not so much. But these believers didn't give up, and neither should you!

If we ask Jesus for advice, he'd probably tell us to ease up a bit. Bashing ourselves doesn't help. With such frenzied routines, it's easy to get distracted. After all, we're only human. He knows our intentions are loving, even if we fall a smidge short.

Building a relationship with God takes time—a lifetime. Our plans may fade for a season, but we renew our promise and start over, continuing a long journey in the same direction toward him.

We are rather like God's turtles. By walking with Jesus, even at tortoise speed, we'll gain an intimacy we never imagined. Slow and steady wins the race.

Search for the LORD and for his strength;
continually seek him.
1 Chronicles 16:11 (NLT)

Be Still
for a
Silent Moment with God

Digging Deeper

Have you tried to adopt a daily prayer practice? How did it go?

How could you be more consistent in your devotional time?

Do you see God in this pursuit? Where?

Prayer for Today

I long to be close to you, God—I really do. But somehow my day gets away from me. Before I know it, I'm headed to bed with scarcely a thought about you. This is not what I want. Help me feel your presence every minute. Guide me on the turtle journey to your arms. Amen.

Your Thoughts

ஒ

Sometimes taking a new route
is the best way to get there.

Out on a Limb

Trust in the LORD with all your heart;
do not depend on your own understanding.
Proverbs 3:5 (NLT)

Do you want your life to matter? Most of us want to do something great. We want to be people of substance, working to better ourselves and our communities. This is an admirable goal. How do we reach it? Where is the "fruit" we passionately seek?

If we desire fruit, first we need an orchard. That's where we'll discover juicy morsels just waiting to be picked, right? Sounds simple, but it's actually more complicated than that.

The problem is, those sweet treats don't actually hang from the tree trunk. We must either climb up and crawl out onto a limb or find a ladder, which may not be very stable. Scaling a ladder or balancing on a branch may be no easy feat. Yet because this crop is important, it's worth the risk.

Going out on a limb in our personal lives is tricky too. We may feel alone. Friends may think we're weird. It may be downright scary. Perhaps that's why most folks don't wander far. They often gather around the trunk instead.

Moving away from the crowd is risky and full of quagmires. But remember—if our goals were easy, they would have been accomplished years ago. Sometimes taking a different route is the best way to get there.

Spiritual challenges are similar. As we earnestly pursue God, the road may lead through briars and brambles. The horizon looks hazy. But he always walks with us, offering more than we ever imagined.

Your goal is worth it. As others view your journey, they can find encouragement to follow their own pathway to Christ. So go out on a limb. Be a fruit-gathering example, and Jesus will meet you there!

Always work enthusiastically for the Lord,
for you know that nothing
you do for the Lord is ever useless.
1 Corinthians 15:58b (NLT)

Be Still
for a
Silent Moment with God

Digging Deeper

What spiritual fruit are you hoping to harvest?

Your goal might involve going out on a limb. How would you handle it?

Where do you see God in this?

Prayer for Today

I want my life to matter. I long to help others and bear fruit for you, God. But I'm afraid of looking different and weird. Let me know that you're walking with me through any hardships I encounter. Together, we can do great things. Hold my hand and let's go! Amen.

Your Thoughts

୬

God's requests may seem impossible.
Yet with his help, we can do it.

Pick Up the Phone

God will make this happen,
for he who calls you is faithful.
1 Thessalonians 5:24 (NLT)

The phone rings. To your surprise, the caller ID reads, "Jesus." Frozen, you stare at the screen. "It can't be him. Why would he call? Will he ask me to do something scary? I don't know what to say."

You let it ring through to voicemail. This hesitation is nothing new. You've doubted your spiritual abilities for years.

Christians just like us have struggled with this dilemma for centuries. We sense that we're called for a special project, but we aren't sure. Maybe it's vanity, wanting others to see us "doing ministry." Maybe we reject our talents, wishing we had more exciting ones. Maybe we are convinced we can't do this work, anyway. Even if we could, who would care?

So we find something—anything—to hold his dreaded request at bay.

It is normal to feel nervous about a difficult task. Sometimes I struggle too, especially with writing. I have to set a kitchen timer to keep my mind focused and my body in the chair.

Are we getting in our own way? Doing a job we aren't meant to do might be far worse than courageously answering the phone. After all, God has confidence in you and me. Even if what he's asking seems impossible, with his help, we can do it.

It's time to pull up our socks, take the call, and get with the program—even if we're scared. Jesus understands. He knows us better than we know ourselves. Watch his eyes sparkle when he hears "hello" on the other end of the line.

Then I heard the voice of the Lord saying,
"Whom shall I send? And who will go for us?"
And I said, "Here am I. Send me!"
Isaiah 6:8 (NIV)

Be Still
for a
Silent Moment with God

Digging Deeper

What is the scariest thing Jesus could ask of you? Explain.

Describe a more likely request. How would you handle it?

Do you perceive God speaking to you about this? In what ways?

Prayer for Today

I don't mean to be stubborn, God, but I'm nervous about what you might ask me to do. What if it's scary? What if I couldn't handle it? I need to calm down and just trust you. Please hold my hand as we walk together into the future you have for me. Amen.

Your Thoughts

൸

Including Jesus in our lives
dramatically shifts our priorities.

The Good Life

Teach me your ways, O LORD,
that I may live according to your truth!
Grant me purity of heart, so that I may honor you.
Psalm 86:11 (NLT)

What do you consider to be the "good life"? It could mean moving to an exclusive neighborhood. Or seeking power and fame. Or relaxing in the lap of luxury. But what does it actually mean to you? Comfort and ease? Prosperity and possessions? Friends and family? Or something else?

Whatever the list, let's not forget the most crucial element—God. But what do we do with him? If he's just an optional add-on, our world may hum along and remain the same. But genuinely including Jesus in our lives can shift our priorities. Former goals lose their appeal.

The early Christians cared little about worldly concerns like riches and status. All that mattered to them was Jesus. In the modern world, such a lofty standard seems outside of our grasp. Modeling our lives after the holy ones of the past is certainly noble, but we also need a realistic framework. Where is the middle ground—the reasonable road to a balanced life?

This quest is influenced by several factors. Age can play a role. Young adults yearn to make an impact, sampling all that society offers. As we approach midlife and beyond, our focus often changes. What we once deemed essential now loses its luster.

Our spiritual path is also a factor. As we draw closer to God, success and wealth pale by comparison. We long to influence others through the example of our faith. What we do matters more than what we have.

Are you ready to redefine the "good life"? Search the horizon of your soul. You'll see Jesus there, beckoning you forward with the answers you seek.

> *I will instruct you and teach you*
> *in the way you should go;*
> *I will counsel you with my loving eye on you.*
> *Psalm 32:8 (NIV)*

Be Still
for a
Silent Moment with God

Digging Deeper

How do you define the good life?

Has it changed over the years? Describe.

In what ways has God influenced your lifestyle?

Prayer for Today

Times change, God, and so do I. In the past, I relished my career success and the trappings that go with it. But their allure has faded, and I'm walking a new path. Today I enjoy a simple lifestyle focused on you. Let's explore the "good life" together. Amen.

Your Thoughts

❧

The authentic life is a
consistent walk toward God.

Tiny Victories

So then, just as you received Christ Jesus as Lord,
continue to live your lives in him . . .
Colossians 2:6 (NIV)

Three of the following ideas are similar. One is not. Can you tell which it is?

Our lives are always problem-free.

Each day overflows with success and abundance.

Living for God is an endless holiday.

Daily life is a grind.

The first three statements sound attractive. Who wouldn't want such a lifestyle? Most of us would be delighted. But it isn't realistic. Did Jesus promise an ideal world full of ease and pleasure? Not hardly! There's no doubt about it—following him is hard work.

The authentic life is about a consistent walk toward God. We strive to do a little better today than yesterday. But it's tough. No one is perfect, and our flaws often get the best of us. Sometimes we're too tired and stressed to even think about our Christian lives.

Yet tiny victories exist. Actually, that's what living for God means. New problems crop up as we zig and zag to stay afloat. Never-ending pressures sap our strength. But look closely. The path to becoming like Christ is alive with small successes. Why not celebrate them?

The sacred journey may be a long, serious, and challenging trek. But don't forget the triumphant moments. Bask in the applause of your spiritual progress. Plant a joyous marker as you scramble along the road.

We might feel as if we're floundering, but Jesus notices. He sees and honors every intention, every small boost in our relationship with him. Even advances that are barely perceptible never escape his attention. After all, he's our biggest fan.

But those who trust in the LORD will find new strength.
They will soar high on wings like eagles.
They will run and not grow weary.
They will walk and not faint.
Isaiah 40:31 (NLT)

Be Still
for a
Silent Moment with God

Digging Deeper

On your road toward Jesus, what tiny victories have you experienced? Describe.

Did you stop to celebrate them? Why or why not?

How do you suppose God views your small victories?

Prayer for Today

What's wrong with my life, God? Why do I struggle? I believe in you, so shouldn't my horizon be filled with sunshine? No, not really. I know better. It's just that I'm frustrated and don't always see the tiny victories we share. Open my eyes to the small graces you shower on me every day. Amen.

Your Thoughts

৵

Is it time to simply chill
and hang out with Jesus?

Another Sleepless Night

Do not be anxious about anything,
but in every situation, by prayer and petition,
with thanksgiving, present your requests to God.
Philippians 4:6 (NIV)

It's one of those nights. After fitfully watching the minutes tick by, at last we fall asleep. But a few hours later, our eyes fly open again. Awake and unable to rest, we obsess over everything we did wrong yesterday.

We toss and turn, fussing about everyday tasks like forgetting to take out the trash or an important detail we missed at work. Spiritual thoughts haunt our minds too. "Why did I blow right past my prayer time tonight?" Or, "How can I be such a slacker in my Bible reading?" It's hard to relax when we feel delinquent about our life with Jesus!

So, is this about God—or us? Does Jesus really demand such slavish devotion? Or are we consumed with trying to earn his favor? When we pray about it, God's answer is always clear. "Don't worry so much." We know he's right, but somehow that doesn't stop the nocturnal nitpicking.

Consider setting aside your incessant doubt and anxiety. Filling your mind with pleasant images of God is comforting and a lot more satisfying. Why not fix your first thought every morning on him? Then, whenever you get a chance, have a quick word with him. I'm sure he'd be delighted!

A pastor once told me our main purpose in life is to glorify God and enjoy him forever. Glorifying is fairly easy. Most of us do that rather well. But enjoyment is another thing entirely. Let's change that.

Maybe it's time to simply chill and hang out with Jesus. Turn off the "internal spiritual task-master" and get a good night's sleep!

Let my soul be at rest again,
for the LORD has been good to me.
Psalm 116:7 (NLT)

Be Still
for a
Silent Moment with God

Digging Deeper

What keeps you awake at night? Describe your concerns.

Are there ways you could stop fretting?

How do you suppose God feels about your worries?

Prayer for Today

Some nights I just toss and turn. Looking at the clock only makes matters worse. My mind is overwhelmed with worries, God. Some are about life. Some are about you. Either way, I need help! Surround me with your calming presence and teach me to let go of these pesky thoughts. Be with me as I drift peacefully off to sleep. Amen.

Your Thoughts

❧

Taking the long view offers
new perspective on our lives.

Walking Uphill

I seek you with all my heart;
do not let me stray from your commands.
Psalm 119:10 (NIV)

"It's all downhill from here." Who hasn't said that after working hard on a project and enduring considerable aggravation? Our bodies and minds are exhausted as we reach the crest of the hill. Finally the job is finished, and now we can coast.

This works well enough for everyday tasks. But what about our spiritual lives? Imagine saying, "I have the religious drill down pat. I'm an expert on the Bible and prayer now, well ahead of my friends. It's time to slack off. No need to go to church anymore. I'm on the downhill side—got it made with God!"

That's preposterous. We don't master the Christian life, then hide it away on a shelf as we pursue more exciting activities. Also, trying to learn everything about our faith in record time, as if this is a race, is a foolish idea. An unhurried pace allows room to grow.

The sacred journey is never an easy, effortless road. But the uphill trek isn't so bad either. With Jesus as our companion, we have infinite opportunities to understand and experience. And don't forget finding ever more delightful ways to nestle in his arms!

Of course, we will encounter seasons of activity and seasons of rest along the path. But when we pause for refreshment, we aren't backsliding. In fact, enjoying a bit of calm and serenity renews our strength.

Taking the long view offers perspective on our lives. Sometimes we're laid low, and Jesus meets us there. During joyous times, we celebrate together with him. But overall, our souls face upward, not down. We walk toward the light streaming from above. Can you see it?

Search for the LORD and for his strength;
continually seek him.
Psalm 105:4 (NLT)

Be Still
for a
Silent Moment with God

Digging Deeper

Have you ever been tempted to just coast downhill in your spiritual life? Describe how that went.

What helped you pick up and move forward again?

How did you perceive God's presence with you?

Prayer for Today

I've worked incredibly hard on my spiritual life, God. Sometimes I feel like slacking off for a bit. But I know that's not how it works. Help me continue walking with you, whether we're scaling high mountains or resting by a cool stream. You and I are in this together forever. Amen.

Your Thoughts

❧

A life of devotion to Christ
requires our full attention.

Playing It Safe

*"'You must love the LORD your God
with all your heart, all your soul,
all your strength, and all your mind.'"*
Luke 10:27a (NLT)

Where do you stand as a Christian? I'm not asking about
doctrines or denominations, but about your faith life with
Jesus. Is it a vibrant, active journey that requires faith and
trust? Where do you stand? Or are you sitting?

A seminar speaker once challenged me: "Too many of
us are content to play it safe. We believe and belong, but we
don't really have to do anything. After we commit to being
Christian, we can safely hide. Nothing is required, nothing
is necessary. We just smile, moving on with our happy lives."

But Jesus didn't play it safe. Neither did his followers,
the holy people of the past. Theirs was a difficult path, filled

with sacrifice but also great joy. In short, they were living for God.

What about us? Is playing it safe our best option? On the surface, it may feel comfortable and effortless. We call ourselves believers. We go to church and mingle. We build friendships and enjoy get-togethers. All the bases are covered, our "I"s are dotted, and the "T"s crossed. Or are they?

By taking the safe route, have we deepened our spiritual growth? Or is it slowly stagnating? A life of devotion to Christ requires our full attention. One-on-one moments with Jesus and knowledge of the Bible are vital. So are deep conversations with others who are well along the road ahead of us. Without serious commitment, our once-blooming faith languishes.

Is it time to shift gears and truly begin living for God? Look! He's up ahead, beckoning you on to the adventure of a lifetime.

I pray that your love will overflow more and more,
and that you will keep on growing
in knowledge and understanding.
Philippians 1:9 (NLT)

Be Still
for a
Silent Moment with God

Digging Deeper

In what ways do you find yourself playing it safe?

Describe what a deeper spiritual life means to you.

How can you walk together with God to reach your goal?

Prayer for Today

I hate to admit this, but I've become lukewarm in my faith. It has been so easy to skate along, doing as little as possible. But that's wrong. You matter to me. Help me experience you more deeply—to hear the words only you can whisper. It's time to make a change and live for you, God. Amen.

Your Thoughts

࿐

See the holy ones of the past,
cheering us on in the race.

Chain Link Fence

I say of the holy people who are in the land,
"They are the noble ones in whom is all my delight."
Psalm 16:3 (NIV)

English theologian John Henry Newman said, "I am a link in a chain, a bond of connection between persons."

At first glance, Cardinal Newman appears to be stating the obvious. Yes, we're all interconnected, and no one is truly alone. In a world of independence and self-sufficiency, this thought brings comfort.

However, there is a spiritual aspect as well. This chain we are part of connects us back 2000 years to the earliest Christians. How uplifting to stand on the shoulders of so many faithful people. Without them, we'd be alone, trying to figure out Christianity by ourselves.

Could such a chain have been a haphazard accident? Perhaps the early followers didn't intend to be linked. But no—the human chain was all part of God's plan. Each person answered his unique call. All of them are treasures, honored through the ages for their strong faith.

So here's a pressing issue: someday we'll be gone, too, and thus become part of the link mesh ourselves. Will we be remembered? Will anyone stand on our shoulders?

It depends. If we walk consistently with Jesus, building a deep and lasting relationship, later believers may be inspired. But if our life and beliefs seem lackluster, they will seek a different set of shoulders.

As we ponder these questions, let us also bask in today's grace. How delightful to be cherished, knowing we are included in God's larger picture. We are never alone. As we run our earthly race, the holy ones of the past are gathered, cheering us on.

Therefore, since we are surrounded by such a
huge crowd of witnesses to the life of faith . . .
let us run with endurance the race God has set before us.
Hebrews 12:1 (NLT)

Be Still
for a
Silent Moment with God

Digging Deeper

Have you been influenced by holy ones of the past? Describe them.

In what ways are you becoming a link on which others can stand?

How do you sense God's plan for you in this chain that spans the ages?

Prayer for Today

I'm so grateful, God, for those who came before me. Their inspiration keeps me going, even on rough days. I want to be a worthy guide for later generations too. Help me become an example as I live the life you've called me to. Amen.

Your Thoughts

୶

Let's quiet our souls to listen
for his still, small voice.

The Fountain

The LORD is in his holy temple;
let all the earth be silent before him.
Habakkuk 2:20 (NIV)

A marble fountain stands in the garden, water slowly filling its upper basin. As the liquid runs over, a steady stream falls through the bowls below, cascading from one to the next. The silence is broken by the gentle murmur of droplets trickling down.

What a lovely and peaceful word picture. The comparison to our Christian spiritual lives is unmistakable. We quiet our souls as we stand before God, calmly listening for his still, small voice. As grace flows through us, we grow ever more focused on him. Soft sounds bathe our senses. Tranquility seeps through the depths of our being, similar to water in a fountain.

Adopting a regular prayer routine is a good way to become like a fountain with its sweet, flowing stream. But it's hard to begin and even harder to sustain. We try—we surely do. But life is busy and unpredictable. By the time evening comes, we are exhausted to the core. Somehow, our best plans went by the wayside.

Consider setting aside a specific time that works for you every day. Some folks enjoy early morning. Others prefer twilight. Whatever you choose, treat it as sacred space—held apart from everyday life. Start with just a few minutes each time, then gradually extend it. Don't overwhelm yourself. Keep it simple. Consistency is the key, always moving ever closer to God.

As we sit with Jesus, he silently saturates our hearts, often catching us by surprise. His love overflows, spilling over into our lives, splashing everyone we meet. We have become the fountain—a never-ending stream of grace.

Let all that I am wait quietly before God,
for my hope is in him.
Psalm 62:5 (NLT)

Be Still
for a
Silent Moment with God

Digging Deeper

Do you have a calming memory of a fountain, or perhaps a flowing stream? Describe.

What feelings does the sound of the moving water bring up in you?

How can you use this experience to be closer to Jesus in prayer?

Prayer for Today

When I sit by a fountain or a small running stream, I feel so peaceful. My soul gradually becomes quiet, calmed by the soothing ripples . Wish you were there with me, God. Oh, wait—you are! Fill me with your life-giving water. Let us be together always in the silent depths of prayer. Amen.

Your Thoughts

Growing with God

＆

Our devotional lives are just
a collection of simple steps.

At the Ballet

My steps have stayed on your path;
I have not wavered from following you.
Psalm 17:5 (NLT)

What do ballet dancers and our spiritual lives have in common?

I once attended a stunning holiday performance of the Nutcracker. As a lover of both music and dance, it's one of my favorites. At this particular performance, something caught my eye. The lavish costumes and lush melodies were beautiful, but the simplicity of the movements fascinated me.

Each section of the dance was based on a series of simple steps. Some were combined in rapid combinations. Others gracefully balanced a slower tempo. The ballet was held together by small moves performed over and over. All were classic lines superbly presented.

Could there be a parallel here? To a new believer, the Christian life looks so complicated. Today a Bible class, tomorrow a prayer group. Then we have Sunday services, the church picnic, and tons of other events. It all sounds exhausting!

Each of these activities is important. Bible study matters. Prayer matters. Gathering together with other believers at church on Sunday matters. How do we boil it all down to the essentials? In reality, our devotional lives are just a collection of simple steps, danced over and over.

We whisper a quick prayer during the day. We spend a few minutes with the Bible. We look forward to a special quiet time shared only with Jesus. It all adds up to a life-long process to deepen our faith and our relationship with Christ.

Whatever our sacred practice, it need not be cumbersome. Laying a cornerstone of simple steps is enough—simple steps leading to God. Who knows, maybe he's watching us dance right now with the tenderest of smiles!

The LORD makes firm the steps
of the one who delights in him…
Psalm 37:23 (NIV)

Be Still
for a
Silent Moment with God

Digging Deeper

What simple steps are important to your faith?

How can you reorganize your life to focus on the basics?

In what ways would these simple steps bring you closer to God?

Prayer for Today

My spiritual life seems so complicated, God. I spend each day running here and there with scarcely a minute to breathe. Is this what you want for me? Maybe faith is simpler than I imagined—just small steps practiced over and over. Show me the way as we sway around the dance floor together forever. Amen.

Your Thoughts

≫

Our example could bring
a thousand folks to Christ.

Put on Your Mask First

But grow in the grace and knowledge
of our Lord and Savior Jesus Christ.
2 Peter 3:18a (NIV)

"Put on your mask first, then assist those traveling with you."
I've heard this instruction over and over as I settle into my
seat before a flight. But who knew it was spiritual advice?

My local coffee shop offers a variety of books for custom-
ers to skim through and hopefully buy. Recently, one caught
my eye—Living in Christ, by Mother Raphaela Wilkinson.
I was struck by her statement, "See to your own salvation
first. Then a thousand around you will also be saved."

Affirming our belief in the gospel is essential, but
committing to spiritual growth matters too. They go
together. As our faith flowers, it blossoms into Christlikeness—a worthy lifetime goal. So, how does this concept

relate to Mother Raphaela's quote?

Christians, especially new ones, love to jump right in with exciting ministry plans. So many souls, so little time. But obstacles may block their progress unless they take care of their own spiritual lives beforehand. Only a deep relationship with Jesus grounds them enough to be a light to others. The deeper the connection, the brighter the flame.

This is good news. The attractiveness of our example could bring a thousand folks to Christ. But in order to let our lamps shine, a consistent devotional life is crucial. That's how we deepen our faith.

The next time the flight attendant tells you to put on your oxygen mask before assisting your companions, remember these words. People are counting on you. They're looking your way for guidance. Don't let them down!

> *...let your light shine before others,*
> *that they may see your good deeds*
> *and glorify your Father in heaven.*
> *Matthew 5:16 (NIV)*

Be Still
for a
Silent Moment with God

Digging Deeper

How would you describe your spiritual "oxygen mask" these days?

What Christian practices are you drawn to?

In what ways are you seeking God as you put on your mask?

Prayer for Today

I have never imagined myself as a leader, God. I don't expect anyone to look to me for spiritual guidance. But maybe I'm wrong. The world longs for your light. Prepare and strengthen me to lead hungry souls to you through my example. Show me how to guide others into your loving presence. Amen.

Your Thoughts

ॐ

When facing the unknown,
let's trust that all shall be well.

God's Math

For I can do everything through Christ,
who gives me strength.
Philippians 4:13 (NLT)

"During my job search, I stepped out in faith and God blessed me with a huge salary." Ever heard this before? Or maybe a friend says, "We trusted in Jesus when we started our business, and he took care of everything. That's just how it works." These are inspiring stories. Suppose they were math equations. We would say our belief plus God's blessing equals exceptional results.

But sometimes the picture isn't so rosy, and situations take a tragic turn. A young pastor and his wife lost a child to a heartbreaking illness. Their friends claimed the little one would have survived if the couples' trust in God had been stronger. Was the equation out of balance?

Spiritual math is problematic. The first examples cast Jesus as a cosmic vending machine, always dispensing anything we want. Perhaps we've re-made him in our image, expecting that he will rubber-stamp every desire and ambition. But is that who he truly is?

And what about the sad endings? Did they really happen because our Christian life was inadequate, mediocre, or worse? Were we slackers in the prayer department? Did we not have enough faith? Or is "enough" even part of God's calculation?

Divine arithmetic is a mystery we can never understand or predict. It's not our responsibility to solve this puzzle. God is not our sugar daddy. Neither is he an impossible taskmaster. He is simply the God who loves us.

When facing the unknown, the best policy is to trust and believe that in the end, all shall be well—whatever that means in God's math curriculum.

And we know that in all things
God works for the good of those who love him,
who have been called according to his purpose.
Romans 8:28 (NIV)

❧

Be Still
for a
Silent Moment with God

Digging Deeper

Does Jesus usually give you what you ask for? What are some examples?

When have you prayed for something you didn't get? Did you ever find out why?

How do you suppose God sees your requests?

Prayer for Today

I realize you're not my cosmic vending machine, God, but sometimes I treat you like one. Then I feel devastated when my prayers aren't answered. I know you want the best for me. Help me understand and trust that you lovingly consider every request. Let me accept your gracious will. Amen.

Your Thoughts

৯

Losing a special person
turns our world upside down.

The Missing Garden Bench

Blessed are those who mourn,
for they will be comforted.
Matthew 5:4 (NIV)

Years ago, our church had a lovely garden bench. It sat on a small stone pavement area, surrounded by an assortment of wildflowers. A narrow path ran past, and often the flowers almost hid the tiny bench. It was a peaceful spot to sit and contemplate the beauty of God's creation.

One day I looked through the church window, and the bench was gone! The flower stalks had been trimmed to the ground. The paving stones were all that remained. The season had changed, and now it was winter. I felt sad. My sweet little bench was missing.

Our sorrow is ever so much deeper when our loved ones pass into the arms of Jesus. Their place is gone. Their bench is missing. All their flowers have been pruned away. We remember their unique essence and how they brightened the landscape of our hearts.

Losing a special person turns the world upside down. Facing overpowering grief is hard, and the healing journey takes time. Some days our mood brightens as we pick up our lives again. Other times are filled with sadness. Yet someone is walking by our side. We might not be aware of his presence. He may speak softly or not at all. But God is there.

No one can escape the loss of a beloved person. Our life seems smaller without them. Yet God is always with us. He never changes. So raise your head. Through your tear-stained eyes, you'll see Jesus longing to enfold you in his compassionate embrace. Go ahead—run and meet him.

The LORD is close to the brokenhearted
and saves those who are crushed in spirit.
Psalm 34:18 (NIV)

Be Still
for a
Silent Moment with God

Digging Deeper

Have you lost someone close to you? What was that person like?

How did you experience a healing journey?

In what ways did you perceive Jesus walking with you?

Prayer for Today

Losing someone special has been one of the hardest experiences of my life. My grief was so intense. Some days I felt lost and had nowhere to turn. Other times I seemed to just crumble. Yet I know you were there, God. You held me up when I couldn't go on. Stay with me as we walk the healing journey together. Amen.

Your Thoughts

୬

Each step we take
brings our spirits closer to God.

A Broken Wing

He will cover you with his feathers.
He will shelter you with his wings.
Psalm 91:4a (NLT)

Some days, we just can't find Jesus. Life struggles weigh us down. Or we feel too defeated to reach out. Whatever the situation, we long to run to him, but simply don't have the strength.

Christian author Matthew the Poor describes it this way:

> *If we tie a bird with a string, he will not be able to fly. If he tries to fly while he is tied, his wing will certainly be broken, and his body will be bruised. If we afterwards untie him, he will not be able to fly. How great the number of souls that could fly toward God were they not fastened to the things of*

this world! It is in vain that man should try to ascend toward God while he is bound with the cords of this earth.

He then notes that we often attempt to fly despite being firmly attached to our worldly cares and commitments. We climb up through the air, believing we're moving toward God. Yet moments later, we slip back, still tethered to what binds us.

Overcoming the troubles that keep us from Jesus is a daunting task. We seem to make progress, only to fall behind again. But all is not lost. Every step carries our spirits nearer to him. Each snapping of the strings of our earthly bonds leads us closer to his loving presence.

Jesus knows our challenges. He sees the sorrow of our hearts, even as he brings a healing balm to the wounded places. We are like tiny birds held in his hand that he lovingly protects and heals. Soon, ever so soon, we'll fly free and unconstrained, headed straight for the heart of God.

"Oh, that I had the wings of a dove!
I would fly away and be at rest."
Psalm 55:6 (NIV)

Be Still
for a
Silent Moment with God

Digging Deeper

What is weighing you down today?

In what ways have you made progress toward "snapping the strings?"

How can you hide under God's wing?

Prayer for Today

I want to be with you, God, yet hurts of the past and issues of today hold me back. I can't seem to get off the ground, no matter how hard I try. Lift me up and teach me to fly straight into your loving arms. Amen.

Your Thoughts

୬

It's best to let go of troubling
memories that hinder our progress.

Don't Look

...but I focus on this one thing:
Forgetting the past and looking forward
to what lies ahead...
Philippians 3:13b (NLT)

A man withdrew to a remote desert area, hoping to focus his life on solitary prayer and God. This was a common practice in the early church. Years later, he received a packet of letters from family and friends. Perplexed, he pondered what to do.

"Should I read them? Will they bring me joy or merely sadness? After such a long time, I fear they would distract me from God. In fact, they already are. My mind wants to look at them. My heart longs to be united with those I've loved. But the quiet, serene life I treasure will be shattered. Would my soul ever find rest again?"

In the end, he chose not to read the letters. He silently threw the bundle into the fire, never looking at the names.

This story is extreme, yet it contains a kernel of truth. We believe our former hurts are healed, and we've moved on. Then a memory pops into our thoughts. Suddenly we're back in those earlier days. Situations play out over and over in our minds—past scenarios we can't change. Finding our footing again is a struggle.

Sometimes it's best to let go of troubling memories that hinder our progress. We've walked many miles since those former times, holding God's hand all the way. However tempting it might be to revisit those thoughts, we may need to leave the past in the past.

So, which is better? Replaying painful images over and over? Or turning them aside to rest our eyes on Jesus? I vote for Jesus!

"Forget the former things;
do not dwell on the past.
See, I am doing a new thing!
Now it springs up; do you not perceive it?"
Isaiah 43:18-19a (NIV)

Be Still
for a
Silent Moment with God

Digging Deeper

Do you replay troubling situations over and over in your mind? How often?

Why do you continue thinking about them?

How might God help you let these thoughts go?

Prayer for Today

It's so hard to release old, painful images, God. I've tried thinking about other things, but the memories jump right back into my mind—like pesky little prairie dogs popping up from their holes. I need your help. Show me how to rid myself of this never-ending cycle. Let me fasten my thoughts on you forever. Amen.

Your Thoughts

≈

What better way to dodge life's turbulence
than by resting in God's arms?

The Still Point

...he leads me beside quiet waters,
he refreshes my soul.
Psalm 23:2b-3a (NIV)

Some days life is overwhelming! When ear-splitting noise invades your senses, how do you cope? When life's pace is too fast, where is your escape? When hiding under the covers doesn't mute the uproar, can your soul ever find peace?

It's time for drastic action. Turn down the volume. Take a break from the high-speed chase. A moment of silence is in order.

But you say, "I've already tried that." You've closed the door and sat quietly, yet your mind didn't stop. It raced back and forth, bouncing off fragments of thought. The gremlins in your brain relentlessly rehashed the events of the day, then amused themselves by dissecting your to-do list for the next three weeks.

Consider taking your mind to the "still point." Rather than focusing on the commotion in your head, drop right through it and rest your attention in the center of your body. The clamor continues up above, but your heart is suspended in quiet.

Of course, this sounds a lot simpler than it really is. Pesky thoughts continue to jump in and divert your mind. One minute, you're basking in silence. The next, you're ruminating on the grocery list. What may have appeared effortless at first now has challenges of its own.

But take courage. A new spiritual practice requires commitment. It's so easy to get distracted. When that happens, quietly return to the silence. Don't feel guilty. Don't give up. Just refocus—over and over.

A discipline like this takes enormous effort. But God— the "still small voice" of Scripture—will nourish your spirit in the calm. What better way to dodge the turbulence than by resting in God's arms?

Be still, and know that I am God!
Psalm 46:10a (NLT)

Be Still
for a
Silent Moment with God

Digging Deeper

Have you experienced the still point? If so, what was it like?

Are you working through the distractions? In what ways?

How has God been with you during these times?

Prayer for Today

Sometimes life is just too much! I need a break, God. A silent time with you sounds wonderful, but quieting my thoughts is rather a challenge. Show me how to find you in the silence. Guide me as I seek your "still small voice" in my noisy world. Let me lay my head on your shoulder and rest. Amen.

Your Thoughts

❧

The most important seeds are
sown directly in other people's lives.

Planting Seeds

...a farmer who plants only a few seeds
will get a small crop.
But the one who plants generously
will get a generous crop.
2 Corinthians 9:6 (NLT)

Is there anything good about aging? Not much! Yet, as we begin that slide toward eternity, we gain a sense of perspective. We now have a longer view, looking back at the results of seeds that were planted, sprouted, and blossomed, often years ago.

Maybe we recall planting a cute little pine tree or a tall, elegant lilac bush. If we still live in the same home, we enjoy the fruit of our labor through restful shade and delicious scents. Even if we've moved on, those plants remain a fond memory that others can now enjoy.

There are many other types of "seeds" to sow. We may plant by starting a business or through volunteering to help those in need. Even a friendly smile can encourage a struggling person.

The most important seeds are sown directly in other people's lives. They could be kernels of faith, encouragement, or even transformation. They might spring up quickly, or they might take 40 years to bear fruit. But everything begins with that first scattering in the ground.

Planting is just the beginning. We can sow a seed that others will water, or we can nurture and care for growth started by someone else years ago. Both are significant. Yet in the end, God makes all seeds grow and flourish.

What seeds are you planting? Are they spiritual ones, bursting forth through the example of your life? Because of you, a delicate blossom may sprout in the heart of a soul in distress. Whatever your situation, it's time to get out the gardening tools and join Jesus, the master grower!

I planted the seed in your hearts,
and Apollos watered it,
but it was God who made it grow.
1 Corinthians 3:6 (NLT)

Be Still
for a
Silent Moment with God

Digging Deeper

Looking back over your life, where have you planted seeds?

Describe how you have seen them grow.

Where is God's hand in your garden?

Prayer for Today

Sometimes I feel as if I have nothing to offer anyone else. But you know that isn't true, God. Even the smallest gesture helps to guide a soul searching for light. Show me how to plant seeds of faith and love while I also nurture those planted by others. Let's garden together! Amen.

Your Thoughts

❧

Set aside your cares for a moment
to rest under God's wing.

Racing Thoughts

"I am leaving you with a gift—
peace of mind and heart.
And the peace I give
is a gift the world cannot give."
John 14:27 (NLT)

Life is busy! We rush to appointments and cram to meet deadlines. We have chores and obligations, and we can't neglect eating and sleeping. No wonder our souls and bodies are on a continual racetrack. Quiet time with Jesus seems out of the question.

This may seem like a 21st century problem, but it's not. Hundreds of years ago, the inspirational Brother Lawrence offered sound advice. He suggested we calm our racing thoughts by holding them close to God's presence. Then the mind becomes relaxed, tranquil, and open to the divine.

Prying our attention away from our circumstances is difficult. We want to focus on prayer, but worries soon intrude. Like a puff of smoke, they can't be contained. When the outside world clamors, any thought of resting in God's presence flies out the window.

Turning our thoughts back to God isn't easy. It requires effort. Here's an idea. Once or twice a day, slip off those imaginary running shoes. Set your cares to the side for a few seconds as you rest quietly under his wing. When reality knocks again, you'll resume your activities a bit more refreshed.

Consider setting aside a short time in your daily routine to intentionally practice this skill. The more you do it, the easier it is to direct your heart to Jesus.

As we periodically give our spirits a brief moment of space, the universe stops spinning so fast. Our hearts become unruffled and more serene when we return to God from time to time during our day. Why not give it a try?

Truly my soul finds rest in God;
my salvation comes from him.
Psalm 62:1 (NIV)

ॐ

Be Still
for a
Silent Moment with God

Digging Deeper

Are you troubled by racing thoughts? When?

What would it take for you to turn your focus toward God's presence?

How might God help you with this?

Prayer for Today

I'm way too busy, God. Distractions and chaos fill each day. My mind runs so fast, I don't think I'll ever catch up. But this isn't the life I envisioned for myself, and it's not what you want for me, either. Help me to slow down and focus on you. Give my soul the peace it has always craved. Amen.

Your Thoughts

When we truly trust God,
whatever he provides is enough.

Enough Is Enough

For where your treasure is,
there your heart will be also.
Matthew 6:21(NIV)

How much is enough? We're talking stuff—clothing, jewelry, tech, money, whatever. How do we know when we have enough? Because "enough" is often a bit more than we already own, it seems we will never have enough.

Living with less these days is rather out of fashion. Some find it silly and naïve. Others believe it's unpatriotic. Experts warn that a decrease in spending will surely sink the economy. Then we'll all be destitute and drown in financial oblivion. But, honestly, how realistic is this economic disaster?

If our motive in sacrificing our personal budgets is not to save the country, why do we press the "buy" button over and over? Maybe we've been taken in by clever ads, designed to plant a desire in our minds. A gaping hole inside us whispers, "fill me." Each new purchase offers the shining hope of happiness. But the dream of finding joy through the things we buy often yields disappointment.

There's more to consider here than our shopping cart fascination. Could we perhaps be crossing a spiritual boundary? When we never possess quite enough and fall short of what we think we need, we are also saying something about God. Where does he fit in our lives—and our purchases?

When we constantly pursue more stuff, we lose the richness of a simple lifestyle. But when we truly love and trust God, whatever he provides is enough. An uncluttered life leaves more room for Jesus. When we aren't pursuing the latest gadget, we discover extra time to be with him and savor his presence. Less is actually more.

> *...for I have learned how to be content*
> *with whatever I have.*
> *Philippians 4:11b (NLT)*

Be Still
for a
Silent Moment with God

Digging Deeper

Do you often crave just a little more stuff? What kinds of things?

How much is enough—really enough?

What lifestyle changes would give you more room for God?

Prayer for Today

Sometimes I feel hopelessly trapped in our consumer society. Slick advertisements say I need something, and I believe them. Whether it's the latest fashion or the coolest tech, I'm hooked. But running up my credit cards isn't a good idea. Today is the day to stop. Help me put on the brakes, God, and simplify my life, so we can spend more time together. Amen.

Your Thoughts

Abiding with God

℘

We are encircled, enclosed, and
encompassed by God's tender affection.

Surrounded

Don't be afraid, for I am with you.
Don't be discouraged, for I am your God.
Isaiah 41:10a (NLT)

Saint Patrick's Day is always a lot of fun. Although many of us love parades, leprechauns, and all things green, there's much more to his story. Even today, Patrick's unique life still speaks to people of faith.

He was born around the year 400 to a wealthy Christian family in Britain. As a teen, he was kidnapped and sold into slavery in Ireland. While tending his owner's sheep, he braved the cold and damp, often without shelter. He wrote about praying at least a hundred times daily and nearly as many through the night. These prayers, he wrote, gave him protection from the ice and snow.

Patrick eventually escaped, yet later returned to Ireland as a missionary. Legend has it that he converted 120,000 people and started 300 churches, all while surviving grave personal danger.

In his innermost being, Patrick knew he was surrounded by Christ. Perhaps you have read his famous prayer: "Christ with me, Christ before me, Christ behind me, Christ in me, Christ beneath me, Christ above me, Christ on my right, Christ on my left…"

What a comforting thought. Wherever we go, Jesus is with us. No matter what our situation, he has it covered. We're never alone. Whether we gaze up or down, right or left, he's there. Everyone is encircled, enclosed, and encompassed by God's tender affection.

Being enveloped by God is a gift. We no longer feel lonely or abandoned in difficult moments. There's no need to search the horizon for help, calling his name. Jesus is always by our side, as close as our very breath.

Yet I am always with you;
you hold me by my right hand.
You guide me with your counsel,
and afterward you will take me into glory.
Psalm 73:23-24 (NIV)

Be Still
for a
Silent Moment with God

Digging Deeper

Have you ever felt surrounded by God's presence? If so, what was it like?

How could you experience that warmth in everyday life?

In what ways might this change your world?

Prayer for Today

Sometimes I feel alone—totally alone. I grope around in the darkness, God, searching for you. But I'm not lost. You're always there, encompassing me with your love and protection. I have nothing to fear. Difficult situations can't hurt me when you enclose me in your grace. Stay with me forever. Amen.

Your Thoughts

℘

Not planning ahead may seem
downright scary.

Soaking Vegetables

We can make our plans,
but the LORD determines our steps.
Proverbs 16:9 (NLT)

Saint Francis never allowed his cook to soak vegetables overnight. Rather, the produce on the following day's menu must be cleaned the same day it was served. The saint literally followed the command of Jesus to "take no thought for tomorrow."

He was braver than most people—especially me. When I read this story, I plunged into an abyss of fear and self-criticism. How would I ever manage without my bank accounts, retirement plans, and investments? With no financial security, how would I be safe?

After I freaked out for a bit, my husband reminded me of another Bible passage in the Book of Proverbs. You know—the one that encourages us to admire the ants because they store up provisions. So, who's right?

I will freely admit that I am an "ant" in disguise. The very idea of not planning ahead seems unwise and downright scary. I suppose a truly holy person would rely solely on God with no concern for the future. But could I do that? Could you?

Saint Francis lived long ago, in a simpler era. Even with our modern social safety net, many today are a single step away from disaster. Of course, God never changes, but situations vary. Perhaps there is a middle ground.

We were born at this particular time in history. In our world, a certain amount of preparation is prudent. How much we depend on those plans may be the key. Do we calculate down to the nth degree, holding fast, no matter what? Or are we flexible and able to follow God's new direction?

Jesus asks that we keep an open hand. Let's start now, letting him guide the way.

Give all your worries and cares to God,
for he cares about you.
1 Peter 5:7 (NLT)

Be Still
for a
Silent Moment with God

Digging Deeper

Do you hold your plans with a firm or loose hand? Explain your approach.

How and when do you make changes?

In what areas can you leave space for Jesus to guide you?

Prayer for Today

I'm a planner, God. My world doesn't feel safe unless I have everything figured out. But then there's no room for you to lead. Help me hold my plans loosely and trust in your guidance. After all, you're the mastermind. It's time to put you back in charge. Amen.

Your Thoughts

৯

With God at our core, we are
protected, sheltered, and secure.

On the Edge

But blessed is the one who trusts in the LORD,
whose confidence is in him.
Jeremiah 17:7 (NIV)

Our faith teaches that God is at the center of all things.
That means everything, including our lives. For many
Christians, this concept can sound dry and academic. As
a result, believers often live on the outer rim of devotion,
twirling round and round toward the outside, never facing
inward toward Jesus.

We flit along the margins, agitated and troubled. Vainly,
we seek to soothe our jangled nerves. But whirling on the
perimeter offers no stability or protective railing. We blow
this way and that, tossing in the wind.

Yet if we courageously turn and walk through the
interior toward the center, the landscape suddenly changes.

Each nervous step brings us closer to our ultimate security. We're no longer off balance. We're not so easily upset. We have peace.

With God at the core, we are protected. We can't fall off the world, because he is everywhere, surrounding us. Nothing exists outside his presence. We are sheltered and secure. Everything is okay. As fourteenth-century Christian mystic and theologian Julian of Norwich wrote, "All shall be well, and all shall be well, and all manner of things shall be well."

Too many of us dance close to the periphery. We allow ourselves to be pulled aside, forgetting that we belong in the center—safe in God's arms. Deep down, we know that his love surrounds our innermost souls. Why would we want to leave such blissful comfort?

It's time to gingerly make a U-turn away from the edge. As we approach the center, there's Jesus, waving up ahead. Let's run into his loving embrace.

"For in him we live and move
and have our being."
Acts 17:28 (NIV)

Be Still
for a
Silent Moment with God

Digging Deeper

Do you often live on the rim of your faith? Describe how.

What causes you the most worry?

How can you move toward the center—and God?

Prayer for Today

I confess, God, that I spend way too much time living on the edge. Maybe I'm nervous about moving toward the center. Or perhaps being with you, up close and personal, seems scary. Help me to get a grip! You are everywhere, and you are love. There's no need to be afraid. Take my hand and lead me right to the middle of your heart. Amen.

Your Thoughts

❧

God's soothing embrace
is always available.

A Soft, Comfy Chair

Then Jesus said, "Come to me, all of you
who are weary and carry heavy burdens,
and I will give you rest."
Matthew 11:28 (NLT)

Some days it just doesn't pay to get out of bed. Troubles we thought were solved yesterday come back to haunt us. Our shoulders bend under the weight of emotional issues, family strife, financial predicaments, and lingering illness. We're overwhelmed with nowhere to turn.

Crawling under the covers again may sound appealing, but it isn't a realistic option. Our burdens and responsibilities will still be waiting for us later. But God offers a special refuge.

While I was on a retreat years ago, a spiritual guide offered some wise advice. "Spend today reclining in God," she said. My assignment was to imagine Jesus as a soft, comfy chair and then lean back and relax, letting him support me.

I spent the day walking around the retreat center grounds, looking for "Jesus chairs." I swayed back and forth in a swing, imagining his loving arms. A rustic bench overlooking a fountain yielded a tranquil moment. Inside the building once more, I nestled up on a couch by the fireside, basking in his tender affection.

God's soothing embrace is always available. As we stretch out, even for a nanosecond, our sense of peace can return. As we rest, a deep calm may overtake our souls. We know we are held, comforted, and loved. All is well.

There will invariably be problems we can't solve and dilemmas that consume our hearts. But we can find a haven in the soft, comfy chair of his presence. Jesus is there, waiting to wrap his arms around us as we snuggle close to him.

In peace I will lie down and sleep,
for you alone, O Lord, will keep me safe.
Psalm 4:8 (NLT)

Be Still
for a
Silent Moment with God

Digging Deeper

Consider resting in a "Jesus" chair. Where could you find one?

What does it feel like to recline in God's soft, comfy arms?

Do you sense his presence with you in this moment? How?

Prayer for Today

Sometimes I just can't go on. I feel fried and need your help, God. And there you are, offering encouragement and cheer. As I relax in your arms, I am supported and safe. I know you'll be there without fail, protecting and caring for me. May I always remember that you "have my back"— literally! Amen.

Your Thoughts

꙰

Let's clean out the mental and
emotional stuff we no longer need.

Filling the Jar

Come close to God,
and God will come close to you.
James 4:8a (NLT)

Some folks are remarkably open to the Holy Spirit. You've seen them. These uncluttered souls are eager to follow wherever God leads. They are attractive, intriguing, and perhaps a bit odd.

Contrast these believers with others who seem stiff and closed. God's voice calls, but they seldom respond. They look busy and productive, but their spiritual core is hollow. How can this be?

Consider a famous illustration about a bag of sand, a box of marbles, and a jar. To meet the goal, every marble and grain of sand must fit in the jar together. The task is harder than it sounds. If we pour the sand in first, the marbles won't all squeeze in. After several attempts, we finally understand that the marbles have to go in first. Then the sand will easily filter through.

Like the marbles in the jar, God can't fully enter a person whose world is packed and brimming over. Jesus longs to be part of our lives, yet he encounters all kinds of obstacles—commitments, jobs, leisure plans, you name it. If the jar is already full, his entrance is blocked. There simply isn't enough space for him.

Perhaps it's time to reassess our priorities. To put Jesus in our jar first, we may need to empty everything else out. Afterwards, we sift in the grains of our various tasks, relationships, and goals around and through him.

If the sand still overflows, then what? It's time to declutter. As we trim back and set aside those unnecessary tasks, a welcoming spot opens in our hearts.

Let's clean out the mental and emotional stuff we no longer need. Soon we'll have lots of space for what matters—God!

"...I am in my Father,
and you are in me, and I am in you."
John 14:20b (NIV)

Be Still
for a
Silent Moment with God

Digging Deeper

Does your world feel cluttered? With what?

Are there physical and emotional items you could get rid of? Describe.

How might putting God in the jar first change your life?

Prayer for Today

I try hard to make room for you, God, but I'm just so busy. The entire world seems to knock at my door. But could I be wrong? Maybe you are the one ringing my doorbell. Help me prioritize and put you first. Let's fill up my jar together. Amen.

Your Thoughts

୬

God accepts our less-than-perfect selves
and always loves us.

A Blank Wall

So God created human beings in his own image.
In the image of God he created them;
male and female he created them.
Genesis 1:27 (NLT)

Johannes Vermeer didn't fit the mold. During the seventeenth century, most painters preferred complex settings. Lush backgrounds featured people of all ages and even animals. But Vermeer was different. The figures in his art—often solitary women—were depicted against a blank or almost empty wall.

His style offers a unique and startling portrayal of the subjects in his artwork. With such a quiet backdrop, their thoughts, emotions, anxieties, and joys are on full display. In a painting, a woman's inner self may radiate through the canvas. Or perhaps her appearance, shrouded in secrecy, invokes a sense of mystery. Either way, our eyes are riveted on the lone figure in the picture.

We face similar challenges today as incessant background noise and advertising bombard us. Our minds are overwhelmed by social media, 24-hour news, and nonstop streaming. When so much hype fills the airways, who knows what's real? But as distractions are stripped away, each soul is highlighted against a blank wall.

In our vulnerability, we reveal God to the world. What do others see? If you stood by yourself in a portrait, would your goodness and light shine through? Would they be overshadowed by a few unattractive traits? If so, that doesn't matter. The image we portray may be tarnished, but God's love can still sparkle through our souls.

Jesus sees you and me with no turbulence or background noise. He accepts our less-than-perfect selves and loves each of us one hundred percent. A simple and transparent life is all he asks, and that's enough.

> *But just as he who called you is holy,*
> *so be holy in all you do...*
> *1 Peter 1:15 (NIV)*

Be Still
for a
Silent Moment with God

Digging Deeper

What does your background wall look like?

If you stripped away the clutter and noise, what would your face express?

What does God see in you that others don't?

Prayer for Today

My world is just too complicated, God. Life is filled with never-ending noise and confusion. I'm drowning in chaos, and I don't want to live that way. Help me restore a simple, quiet heart. Place me against the clean, cozy background of your canvas. As I reflect your image, let your light shine through to all around me. Amen.

Your Thoughts

৶

Faith is knowing in the silent depths
of our being that Christ is real.

Simple Faith

Then Jesus said,
"Did I not tell you that if you believe,
you will see the glory of God?"
John 11:40 (NIV)

Either we believe, or we don't. It's that simple. Or is it? Statements like these are often challenged in today's world. Is the belief scientific? Is it logical? Can it be proven? Is it consistent with archaeological findings? Or do these issues even matter?

Simple faith is knowing in the silent depths of our being that Christ is real. We feel no need to question, no need to explain inconsistencies, no need to prove a case. Deeply experiencing God is all that is necessary. Either we believe, or we don't.

Some of us grew up in Christian families and knew Jesus from the beginning. Others were raised in homes of different beliefs or none at all. I was a child in a non-Christian family. In my home, religion, if it existed at all, had to make logical sense. But after accepting Christ in mid-life, concerns about a provable faith slowly receded from my thoughts and no longer troubled me.

Perhaps we've discovered the secret known by devout men and women down through the ages. Many faced great trials and hardship, yet they endured. Each experienced a deep spirituality that simply loved and accepted God, no questions asked. They truly rested in him and found peace beyond understanding. Their stories inspire and uplift our inner beings. We want what they had.

As we walk with Jesus through the years, our souls understand that simple faith is all we need. May we always rest in his arms, safely next to his heart, together forever.

May the God of hope fill you
with all joy and peace as you trust in him,
so that you may overflow with hope
by the power of the Holy Spirit.
Romans 15:13 (NIV)

Be Still
for a
Silent Moment with God

Digging Deeper

What is your definition of simple faith?

How can you attain this?

What would it feel like to be enfolded in God's arms?

Prayer for Today

I long for the simple faith of the believers of earlier times. Sometimes it's so hard, God. Doubts creep in. Others mock me, demanding scientific proof. Some days I want to give up, yet I know you're with me. I feel you. I sense your loving presence. Help me walk with you in humble and quiet trust forever. Amen.

Your Thoughts

୭

Our eternal flame never goes out,
regardless of the situation.

Eternal Flame

The light shines in the darkness,
and the darkness has not overcome it.
John 1:5 (NIV)

Have you ever seen an eternal flame? It's a small fire that never goes out. Since these are mainly found at grave sites, we rarely talk about them. A friend of mine once compared her faith to such a flame. "Sometimes the blaze burns hot and strong. Other times I scarcely notice it. But a faint glow is always there."

How true! Some days, we're bold and passionate, ready to live the Christian life to the max. Our prayers are supercharged, and our ministry work flourishes. Everything we touch turns to gold, and our world is rosy and bright. All is well.

But there are also difficult seasons. We feel tired, worn out, discouraged, and depressed as day after day drags on.

The fire sputters and shrinks to almost nothing while we barely muddle through. Gloomy drizzle clouds our view with no rainbow in sight. At times, the spiritual life doesn't seem to be worth the trouble.

This contrast has been known through the ages as consolation and desolation. Even the most seasoned saints experience this cycle, yet they carry on. The dark night of discouragement does not deter them. Instead, they wait for the warm sense of renewal to return. Energized again, enthusiasm fills their souls.

Our eternal flame is never extinguished, regardless of the situation. Even in our darkest moments, a tiny flicker guides our hearts along the way. Then, ever so slowly, the spark begins to spread. As it expands to a golden beam, what do we see? Jesus is holding out his arms, beckoning us forward. Let's walk together in the light.

> *"And be sure of this:*
> *I am with you always,*
> *even to the end of the age."*
> *Matthew 28:20b (NLT)*

Be Still
for a
Silent Moment with God

Digging Deeper

Describe your eternal flame. Is it a dazzling light, barely visible, or a little of both?

How do you cope with the ups and downs of Christian life?

Where do you find God in your struggles?

Prayer for Today

Some days, the brightness of my faith almost blinds me, God. Other times, I barely notice a flame among the smoking embers of my heart. But I know it's still there. Give me strength to walk through the difficulties I face. With you by my side, this sacred spark will emerge and grow once more. Amen.

Your Thoughts

❧

A golden thread runs through
every soul—even yours.

Essence of Life

You will show me the way of life,
granting me the joy of your presence
and the pleasures of living with you forever.
Psalm 16:11 (NLT)

What is a life well lived? What is an authentic Christian self? What is our sacred essence—the flame that burns deep within each of us?

The death of a dear friend led me to ponder these questions. As a ministry leader, she lovingly guided a congregation of struggling and disadvantaged souls. She listened to and affirmed each one. She stood beside those seeking justice, her courage on full display.

My friend wasn't rich or famous as she labored in obscurity. Her legacy lives mostly in the memories of those she loved. But hers was a life well lived. She spent her days standing for what was right and caring for those who needed help. Christ was the light at the center of her being, and she remained a golden thread in his tapestry.

What about your story? What direction are you going? Does a particular ministry grab your heart? Perhaps you sense Jesus beckoning you forward, drawing you in. As you move through the seasons of life, he is laying down tracks for you to follow. His gentle hand guides you in living out your unique contribution.

Spiritual growth is a long process. It can take years to understand your special identity—what you stand for and what you believe. The road may turn many corners as you overcome obstacles and identify new gifts. Yet this is a journey worth taking. If you patiently search, you will discover your personal essence.

A golden thread runs through every soul—even yours. Experience the joy of walking hand-in-hand with Jesus as he weaves you into his eternal tapestry.

> *…he who began a good work in you*
> *will carry it on to completion…*
> *Philippians 1:6b (NIV)*

Be Still
for a
Silent Moment with God

Digging Deeper

Have you discovered the essence of your life? If so, what is it?

How do you hope to be remembered?

In what ways are you working with God to make this a reality?

Prayer for Today

Sometimes I think I understand what you want for my life, God, but other times I'm baffled. I know you have wonderful and exciting plans for me. Show me the way and reveal the legacy you have for me. Help me become a golden thread, just right for your divine loom. Amen.

Your Thoughts

ℂ

Saying yes to God's requests
can be a scary proposition.

Wilt Thou Refuse?

*Then I will sing praises to your name forever
as I fulfill my vows each day.*
Psalm 61:8 *(NLT)*

Mother Teresa has been a much-loved figure throughout the world for decades. Countless articles, books, and films have documented her story and mission. Yet here is one little-known fact about her. Before starting her work with the destitute in India, she took a solemn vow. She promised Jesus that she would never refuse anything he asked.

Earlier in life, she taught at a convent school. After hearing God's call, she began the lengthy process of setting up the Missionaries of Charity. Early on, an insistent inner voice kept asking, "Wilt thou refuse?" In time, she honored her pledge. Her legendary devotion to the poor flowed from a holy promise made long before.

Would you make such a vow? To give yourself to God, doing only what he asks, is the ultimate in spiritual selflessness. Being a vehicle for his will is a worthy goal, but it can be scary too. What if you don't like his request? You couldn't back out on your vow. You'd be stuck!

How would you prepare for such a commitment, assuming you are game to try it? Consider these suggestions:

First, strengthen your trust in Jesus. Is he reliable? Does he lead you? Has he been there for you? As you search your heart and memory, the answers will appear.

Then listen for his voice. The gift of truly hearing God is vital. It takes time to identify his voice, hear his direction, and then follow through. Once you build confidence in his guidance, making the promise is the final step.

Vows are serious. So is committing to do whatever God asks of you. Could you do it? Would you do it?

"When you make a vow
to the LORD your God,
be prompt in fulfilling
whatever you promised him."
Deuteronomy 23:21a (NLT)

Be Still
for a
Silent Moment with God

Digging Deeper

Have you considered making a solemn promise to God? Describe it.

How would you prepare?

In what ways would you seek God's help?

Prayer for Today

Never saying no to you, God, sounds scary. I'm not sure I really want to do it. Being in control of my life and doing whatever I choose is attractive. Take my hand and give me courage. Guide me as you keep me under your protective wing. Be with me as I make my sacred vow. Amen.

Your Thoughts

The Journey Continues

Being hidden in God's heart is delightful, and it can be challenging too. Friends and family might think we're weird. We ourselves may feel rather overwhelmed. But the rewards outweigh the difficulties. After all, Jesus is always with us. In stressful times, he's right there, holding our hands, whispering words of comfort.

As we settle into God's heart, let's ponder one of his best attributes. He is faithful. Whether our lives are going swimmingly or in tatters, he always reaches out, expressing his love. He longs to shelter us under his wing. Scripture and a much-loved hymn offer this reminder:

> *Great is his faithfulness;*
> *his mercies begin afresh each morning.*
> *Lamentations 3:23 (NLT)*

These reassuring words are a balm for our souls. Each day presents new possibilities. Each day offers tender mercies. Each day is secure in his faithfulness.

In these 40 reflections, you have searched the inner chambers of God's heart. Together you toured his house and explored every inch, from the gazebo to the attic hideaway. But what's next? As you continue to nestle in his heart, be sure to take time to venture out. Be an example to those seeking faith. Show them the way to Jesus. But no matter how far you roam, remember that your heart is intertwined with his. Come back home.

The road to a close relationship with God isn't easy. It's strewn with detours, potholes, barricades, and fallen trees. But you have a love for him, a heart that seeks his. Whatever the issue, you're up to it.

The Bible provides encouragement for the journey. As you consider your next steps, let these words wash over you.

> *Surely your goodness and love*
> *will follow me all the days of my life,*
> *and I will dwell in the house of the LORD forever.*
> *Psalm 23:6 (NIV)*

As our devotional time draws to an end, let's offer a simple prayer.

Being with you means everything, God. I long to be close to you, to stroll through your home, to nestle in your heart. Thank you for being with me on this journey. You've offered love, guidance, and encouragement as I grow ever closer to you. Let us walk together, hand-in-hand and heart-in-heart, forever. Amen.

May the peace of the Lord be always with you.

About the Author

Lisa Aré Wulf is an award-winning women's devotional author. Her print, audio, and e-books have been finalists in the USA Best Book Awards, the Independent Author Network Book of the Year Awards, the Next Generation Indie Book Awards, and the Voice Arts Awards.

Publications across the country have featured Lisa's articles on Christian living and spiritual growth. As a speaker, she shares her faith journey with transparency and grace.

A graduate of Fuller Theological Seminary, Lisa also holds two degrees from the University of Colorado. She is an adjunct accounting professor, owned a CPA firm, served in elected public office, and was a professional orchestral musician.

Lisa lives in Colorado with her husband, Calvin. They have four children and are happy empty nesters.

For more information about Lisa Aré Wulf, please visit LisaAreWulf.com.

Made in the USA
Las Vegas, NV
21 October 2023

79463417R00111